Ministry
of Hospitality

Sylvia Cirone Deck

Santa Clara University
Pastoral Ministries Program
Sheed & Ward
Kansas City

Sheed & Ward™ is a service of The National Catholic Reporter Publishing Company.

ISBN: 1-55612-951-3

Published by: Sheed & Ward
                115 E. Armour Blvd.
                P.O. Box 419492
                Kansas City, MO 64141-6492

To order, call: (800) 333-7373

Contents

Acknowledgments

I am grateful for the support of my husband, Jerry, and our children. I am also indebted to the faculty of the Graduate Program in Pastoral Ministries at Santa Clara University, especially Sr. Rita Claire Dorner, O.P. and Sr. Anne Marie Mongoven, O.P., and my parish family at Holy Cross Church in Santa Cruz, California. The rich experiences of family gatherings and ritual provided by my Italian heritage have also been blessings.

Introduction

Just as the bread broken
was first scattered on the hills,
then was gathered and became one,
so let your Church be gathered
from the ends of the earth into your kingdom,
for yours is glory and power through all ages.[1]

Christians are those people who, through the ages, have been called by God and who have responded by gathering together. The early church, described in *Acts*, began as an assembly of disciples "gathered in one place" (Acts 2:1). When the day of Pentecost came, the disciples, filled with the Holy Spirit, added to their number by baptizing thousands. These early Christians "devoted themselves to the apostles' instruction and the communal life, to the breaking of bread and the prayers" (Acts 2:42). The richness and simplicity of Christian tradition as expressed in the New Testament is underscored by the words of the third Eucharistic Prayer: "From age to age you gather a people to yourself, so that from east to west a perfect offering may be made to the glory of your name."[2]

The glory of God's name is experienced in the midst of the community gathered for worship. It is at worship, "where two or three have gathered" in his name, that Christ is "in their midst" (Matthew 18:20); it is at worship that those acting in his name manifest the power of the Spirit (1 Corinthians 12-14); it is from worship that those going forth to preach the Gospel are sent (Acts

13). Believers renew themselves (Romans 12:1), and those seeking Baptism come to make their petition at worship (Act 2:38).[3]

Within the gathered community, the People of God are challenged to holiness and dedication. The documents of the Second Vatican Council, recognizing the significance of the community gathered for worship, reflect a "shift in Roman Catholic approach to worship" from the priest as the principal celebrant to "the general role of the congregation as the principal one . . ."[4]

This shift in the approach to worship can also be noted in the *Constitution on the Sacred Liturgy*, 1963. In this document "the order of presenting modes of Christ's presence is from his presence in the eucharistic species to a presence in the believing community, 'where two or three are gathered together in my name'." (CSL, 7). This order, however, is reversed in the later encyclical on the Eucharist: *Mysterium fidei* of 1965 (nos. 35-38) and *Instruction on Eucharistic Worship* of 1967 in which the starting point for Christ's presence is the believing community.[5]

The *General Instruction of the Roman Missal*, published in 1969, states clearly and emphatically that "The celebration of Mass is the action of Christ and the people of God . . . " and that as such, "it is the center of the whole Christian life." (GIRM, 1) Such actions as gathering together, listening to the word of God, sharing the Eucharist and going forth to bring the good news to the world do more than provide the framework of liturgical celebration; they are the essence of the celebration.

The actions of the Mass join the people of God in worship "through the ages" with those early Christian assemblies who experienced Christ coming among them in simple human actions of mutual hospitality. Early Christian worship flowed from the awareness of the presence of Christ in such ordinary actions as comforting the sick, washing one another's feet, opening their arms to strangers and sharing "the common food and drink of the Body and Blood in the forms of bread and wine."[6]

It is time to reclaim the power of these simple acts of hospitality in the liturgy. For nearly one thousand years people have been passive observers at liturgy. Although the Second Vatican Council has invited the People of God to become active participants once again, many remain oblivious or are hostile to the active role of the assembly in celebration. Since a declared objective of liturgical reform is to bring about "that full, conscious, and active participation in liturgical celebrations called for by the very nature of the liturgy,"[7] the primary task of liturgical renewal is to bring the worship of parishes to life. The only energy that has the power to do so, claims Eugene Walsh, is hospitality.[8]

Hospitality is more than a concept; it is an attitude of the heart, a way of being that defines the Christian life. Hospitality, a creative force vital to our Christian condition, is the act of making room for others in our hearts and in our communities. The accomplishment of such an elusive activity in a parish setting is challenging.

PURPOSE OF THIS BOOK

Every ministry requires mutual support and spiritual growth, but resources and guidance for developing a ministry of hospitality appear to be minimal in many parishes. For instance, while ministers of the word and eucharistic ministers generally receive training and guidance in their ministries, it seems that ushers and greeters, whose ministry is vital to liturgical celebration, appear to receive only token attention. Our purpose here is, therefore, to present a liturgical catechesis for developing the ministry of hospitality in the parish setting. Based on a theological foundation and principles of catechesis, the process seeks to prepare ministers of hospitality for service to the community gathered for worship as well as bring participants to new levels of experience as members of the assembly.

SOURCES

The primary sources for this paper include the Vatican II documents *Constitution on the Sacred Liturgy* and *Decree on the Apostolate of Lay People* as well as the liturgical documents *General Instruction of the Roman Missal* and *Environment and Art in Catholic Worship.* Also included are *The Sacramentary, The Lectionary for Mass* and such early Church texts as "The Acts of the Apostles" and "The Didache." *Sharing the Light of Faith, National Catechetical Directory for Catholics of the United States,* Joseph Cardinal Bernardin's pastoral letter on liturgy, *Our Communion, Our Peace, Our Promise,* and *Liturgy,* the journal of The Liturgical Conference, provide additional resources. Much inspiration and valuable insights were gleaned from books by Henri Nouwen, James Dallen, David N. Power, Ralph A. Keifer and Robert Hovda, as well as articles by Eugene Walsh, Phillippe Rouillard, Regina Kuhn and Kenneth Smits and by the North American Forum on the Catechumenate.

Interviews with the pastor and liturgist at Holy Cross Church in Santa Cruz, California furnished experiential data. Their unique perspective and hopes for Holy Cross Church were a basic consideration in the design and implementation of the process.

METHODOLOGY

The catechetical sessions designed to initiate the ministry of hospitality form the core of this paper. They owe their inspiration to the catechetical process taught by Sr. Rita Claire Dorner in Pastoral Liturgy and Sr. Anne Marie Mongoven, O.P. in Catechetics. Guided by their vision for the Church, the sessions reflect the substance and spirit of their teachings.

The sessions flow from an understanding of hospitality considered at three levels: human, biblical and liturgical. Each of these approaches to an understanding of hospitality is developed in light of its meaning for the new ministry. The catechetical process is described from varying perspectives. First, the consideration of hospitality as a ministry is explored. Then, the four tasks of catechesis are outlined and developed in relation to the four sessions: building community through the process, reflecting on the stories and beliefs of the participants, serving each other and those beyond the walls of the church and praying together at each session. The format of the process, its basic shape and flow, is then described.

Finally, the groundwork for initiating the new ministry in the parish is presented, and promotion of the process, based on studies of adult participation in educational opportunities, is described. The final design of the process is based on all of the preceding considerations. Questions of where, when and how the process would be presented are answered in the conclusion of the section on the Catechetical Process.

OVERVIEW

This study includes three sections: (1) an explication of the nature of hospitality, (2) a description of the catechetical process, and (3) a detailed plan for each of the four sessions. A concluding statement examines the process in the light of its catechetical goals and theological implications. Appendix A includes an example of a commissioning rite.

ONE

The Nature of Hospitality

We have all experienced hospitality but we may not have thought aobut it very much. In this section we will consider the nature of hospitality from three perspectives: the human dimension of hospitality, the biblical tradition from which hospitality flows and the liturgical experience of hospitality. An understanding of these three elements forms the basis of a catechesis for hospitality ministry.

THE HUMAN DIMENSION OF HOSPITALITY

Hospitality is foundational to the understanding of human life. It is an integral component of all social gatherings, beginning when families gather around the table and share their lives as well as their meals. The table is the place where family members seek and find nourishment, fellowship, comfort, wholeness, and identity. In their daily gatherings for physical nourishment families stay in touch with each other's activities and concerns. They listen and respond to each other as they express joys and sadness, hopes and fears. As they gather at the family table, sharing their stories, embraces and laughter, they *become* family.

The meal becomes an even greater sign of the commonality and unity which characterizes hospitality when the extended family joins in celebration of such special events as birthdays and anniversaries, Thanksgiving and Christmas. Together the family is linked to its past through memories. It shares in the events of the present and builds a foundation for future family gatherings and memories. It does so through its stories and such familiar signs as decorations, candles on a cake, songs and other family rituals.

When guests are invited to share in these meals, the family becomes community, extending itself beyond itself to enfold others. In the sharing of its meal and its home, the family is sharing everything that makes it a family. What gives form to all of these gatherings are the expressions, the signs and gestures, of hospitality.

Karl Rahner, in his essay on "The Theology of the Symbol," states that all beings are by nature symbolic. In order to attain their nature, they have to "express" themselves.[9] One may conclude from this statement that when human self-expression takes shape through the dynamics of hospitality, human beings are forging the elements of community. This means that when an individual or a family opens its doors to guests, it expresses itself through the signs of hospitality. The family offers food and drink and provides an environment of comfort and relaxation through such special touches as music, flowers, candles or a fire in the fireplace. The family's actions are signs of its caring as family members smile and embrace visitors, making room for them and giving them full and loving attention. As the family shares its food and drink, its stories and rituals, it shares its life.

Hospitality sets the stage for interaction, dialogue and intimacy. It promotes a sense of unity and peace where both host and guest experience freedom. Just as family members feel free to be who they are and become who they want to be, guests also find freedom to become part of something greater than themselves. Henri Nouwen explains that "hospitality is not to change people, but to offer them space where change can take place." Hospitality is "the creation of a free space where the stranger can enter and become a friend . . ."[10]

The practice of hospitality finds its source and strength in biblical tradition. Hospitality is by no means a new idea. The scriptural heritage of the people who gather provides inspiration and direction for their work of reaching out and gathering in.

THE BIBLICAL TRADITION OF HOSPITALITY

The biblical tradition is rich in examples of hospitality. For instance, when Abraham invited three strangers in from the desert to share his food and drink, he had no idea that this familiar and simple gesture of hospitality would bring such startling changes to his life (Genesis 18:1-15). His response was the customary one of sharing all that one has with strangers. Abraham ran forward to greet them and implored them to stay; he "hastened" to Sarah, instructing her to bake rolls. He "ran" to pick out a choice steer from his herd. His movements were urgent, deliberate and caring. His full attention was on the unexpected guests brought to his tent.

Although the prospect of entertaining angels probably never occurred to Abraham, the strangers in his care were certainly treated as such. In the midst of desert heat, thirsty, hungry and tired, they were given refreshment. They were asked to bathe their feet and rest while their host waited on them. This was sweet reward, indeed, for their hardships. The author of Hebrews probably had this story in mind when he urged his readers to "love your fellow Christians always. Do not neglect to show hospitality, for by that means some have entertained angels without knowing it" (Hebrews 13:1-2).

The widow of Zarephath offered shelter and food to Elijah, giving him the last of her meager food supply. Like Abraham, her generous gesture brought a rich and unexpected reward, for Elijah revealed himself as a man of God by giving her abundant oil and flour and later raising her son from the dead (1 Kings 17:9-24).

In the parable of the prodigal son in the New Testament, both the son and his father experienced the potential of hospitality in a rich and rewarding manner. The father, throwing his arms around his son's neck and kissing him, called for fine robes and rings, orders that a fatted calf be killed and a celebration begun (Luke 15:11-32). The astonishment of the younger son at this unexpected and overwhelming welcome must have surpassed the dismay of his older brother. Through the actions of hospitality, the father expressed his unconditional love. Both he and his son were blessed.

When two travelers on the road to Emmaus invited a fellow traveler to spend the night with them, the stranger made himself known to them as their Lord and Savior in the breaking of the bread (Luke 24:13-35). Their hospitality brought them unexpected blessings.

The "evocative potential" of hospitality expressed in these stories, Henri Nouwen concludes, "can deepen and broaden our insight in our relationships to our fellow human beings."[11] Both Hebrew Scriptures and the New Testament tell us not only how serious is the obligation to welcome strangers but also that guests carry "precious gifts with them which they are eager to reveal to a receptive host."[12] When fear and distrust are converted into hospitality, then " the distinction between host and guest proves to be artificial and evaporates in the recognition of the new found unity."[13] Is it possible that in the act of hospitality both host and guest incorporate angelic qualities?

Are each blessed? Jesus suggested as much in Matthew's Gospel account of the last judgment when the king spoke to those on his right: "Come. You have my Father's blessing! . . . I was a stranger and you welcomed me" (Matthew 25:31-46).

The Canaanite woman provides a provocative image for the issue of access, that is, who is welcomed and who is rejected (Matthew 15:21-28). Hospitality is not a matter of simply opening the door and allowing the Canaanite woman or man or child to enter; it is a matter of actively seeking them out and inviting them in, for without them, we are lost."[14] The Canaanite woman demands action; the Gospel demands it. When the disciples asked Jesus where he lived, he did not simply tell them; he said, "Come and see" (John 1:39). Those who practice hospitality are consecrated by their baptisms to go out and invite others to "come and see."

Additional biblical images of hospitality are found in the persons of two friends of Jesus, Martha and Mary. Martha is the organized, well-prepared hostess. "Busy with all the details of hospitality," she attended to her guests' comfort and nourishment (Luke 10:38-42). However, Mary, her sister, neglected the "household tasks" to sit at Jesus' feet and listen to his words. When Martha complained, the Lord pointed out that "one thing only is required. Mary has chosen the better portion and she shall not be deprived of it." Jesus made it clear that the primary task of hospitality, the whole-hearted attention to the guest, was being satisfied very well by Mary. Hospitality was engineered by Martha; it was energized by Mary. Both were necessary.

A final intriguing biblical image of hospitality is provided by John the Baptizer. He prepared the way of the Lord. Preaching repentance, his passion was contagious. Those who gathered to hear him and to be baptized in the waters of the Jordan River were so moved by his speech and manner that many believed he was the promised Messiah. But John made it clear that "the one who will follow me is more powerful than I . . ." (Matthew 3:11). John's preaching and style set the stage, preparing the people for the one whose sandals he was "not even fit to carry." John gave witness to a generous and loving heart, a heart that had been emptied to make room for the other, and a willingness to accept and seek out the alienated, hurting, disenfranchised and poor. John was the perfect host.

An understanding of the biblical witness of John, Martha, Mary, the travelers to Emmaus, the widow of Zarephath and Abraham enriches the hospitality practiced at home. When such an understanding of hospitality is translated into liturgical experience, then hospitality is not only facilitated but makes sense.

THE LITURGICAL EXPERIENCE

The Incarnation tells us that Christ emptied Himself and entered into the human condition (Philippians 2:7). That human condition is found in the community which gathers for worship on the Lord's Day. The community is the living sign of Christ among us, the living sign of His humanity and divinity. Through its worship together, the community expresses Christ's life, death and resurrection and in doing so, enters into relationship with God. The document *Environment and Art in Catholic Worship* states:

Incarnation, the paschal mystery and the Holy Spirit in us are faith's access to the transscendence, holiness, otherness of God. An action like liturgy, therefore, has special significance as a means of relating to God, or responding to God's relating to us. . . . God has graciously loved us on our own terms, in ways corresponding to our condition. Our response must be one of depth and totality, of authenticity, genuineness, and care. (EACW, 13)

This statement has everything to do with hospitality as it is exercised in liturgy. The document further describes the "experience of mystery which liturgy offers in its God-consciousness and God-centeredness" in the following statement:

This [experience of mystery in liturgy] involves a certain beneficial tension with the demands of hospitality, requiring a manner and an environment which invite contemplation (seeing beyond the face of the person or the thing, a sense of the holy, the numinous, mystery). A simple and attractive beauty in everything that is used or done in liturgy is the most effective invitation to this kind of experience. One should be able to sense something special (and nothing trivial) in everything that is seen and heard, touched and smelled, and tasted in liturgy. (EACW, 12)

In other words, the experience of liturgy is very much like the experience of those invited into loving homes or the experience of Abraham greeting the three strangers or the prodigal son welcomed by his father's unconditional love. There is nothing halfhearted in the gesture of hospitality. It is an action in which, as stated above, "one should be able to sense something special. . ."

This "something special" is what a ministry of hospitality brings to the liturgy. Hospitality begins with a predisposition or an attitude of care towards others, like Abraham's. According to Regina Kuehn, hospitality begins "when we move beyond our solitary self and decide to become lifegivers for others."[15] It begins in our bodiliness, our gestures. It begins, in fact, in the simple gesture of open arms.

The ministry of hospitality requires an authentic, genuine and caring response to the needs of everyone who gathers. It requires sensitivity, openness and a willingness to risk losing oneself in order to find oneself (Matthew 10:39), for, as Nouwen writes, it is a "poverty of heart that makes a good host."[16] To invite another into a new relationship requires that "weeds and stones" be gently removed in order that change can take place within the love of the community.[17]

The development of a consciousness of hospitality depends on what Ralph Keifer calls a "baptismal spirituality." He defines such spirituality as "the development of a Catholic lay consciousness of mission in the world as a consecrated people."[18] The "renewal of liturgical life," he maintains, is "integrally and organically related" to such development.[19] Christians must understand themselves, in other words, as being consecrated through their baptism for service to the world. The recovery of such spirituality in the praying assembly, Keifer concludes, is "the restoration of the assembly's sense that it is Christ the Lord who is present by the very fact of the baptized having gathered together."[20]

It is a contention of this project that the ministry of hospitality is a powerful means for the assembly's perception of itself as "a mode of Christ's presence."[21] The ministers, aware of themselves as consecrated for their task through their baptism, are models of Christ present in the assembly. They bring an energy and focus to worship which can pervade the community like leaven lightens "the whole mass of dough" (Matthew 13:33). The subtleties of hospitality bring new life and spirit to the worship assembly and to relationships within that assembly. It does not need to be told it is "Christ the Lord who is present by the very fact of the baptized having gathered together."[22] The assembly experiences it through the dynamics of hospitality.

Clear demands are made, therefore, upon ministers of hospitality. The burden of achieving unity, wholeness and health in the parish setting rests upon those who extend welcome: the presider, liturgical ministers, specifically the ministers of hospitality, both greeters and ushers, and the assembly. All must be willing to reach out and embrace everyone who comes through the doors of the church. It is an indiscriminate embrace; one cannot choose to welcome one person and not another. The all-embracing love of Christ gathers everyone to Himself. There is no other way to preach the Gospel than to do the same.

Finally, in *Gathering for Eucharist*, James Dallen writes that each person who enters the place of worship contributes to the action of gathering "if that person and those who follow make room for one another and make one another welcome. Only in this way will they become community rather than a crowd of individuals."[23] The recognition of one another as members of a celebrating community is vital to a ministry of hospitality. The action of gathering initiates and establishes a sense of unity and belonging which is expressed through the actions of listening, sharing and going forth to spread the message. If these primary actions of the assembly are to be "unified and purposeful," then the community must have experienced itself as welcomed and welcoming. "Hospitable, welcoming interaction is essential" during the action of gathering.[24]

A theology of hospitality which promotes openness and space for the other is at the core of the Christian message. All of the ways that hospitality or welcome are experienced in community are manifestations of the dynamics of Christ's presence. As Henri Nouwen states: "To help, to serve, to care, to guide, to heal" are words "used to express a reaching out toward our neighbor whereby we perceive life as a gift not to possess but to share."[25]

In summary, liturgy "flourishes in a climate of hospitality: a situation in which people are comfortable with one another . . ." (EACW, 11) It is a situation where there is no distinction between host and guest. Regina Kuehn states:

> When the parish assembles for Sunday worship it makes visible the body of Christ. . . To detect differences and to dwell on them is the most common daily experience, but to savor our commonness and to create unity – that is an art, that is the art of hospitality.[26]

CONCLUSION

In this presentation, hospitality as an art will be explored through the dynamics of the catechetical outlined in four sessions. The sessions flow from an understanding of hospitality as it is experienced in human life, as it is found in biblical tradition and as it is expressed in liturgical celebration. They aim at helping parishioners experience hospitality on two levels: as those who are received and embraced and those who reach out to enfold the other into the midst of its body, the Body of Christ, the parish community.

TWO

The Catechetical Process

HOSPITALITY AS A MINISTRY

Bartimaeus, the blind beggar in Mark 10, and the Canaanite woman in Matthew 15 would encounter some difficulty trying to join those gathered for Sunday worship in most churches. As one writer points out, Bartimaeus would be escorted outside or to the "cry room,"[27] while the Canaanite woman would be asked, no doubt, to hold her peace and make an appointment with the pastor. The primary concern of those at the door would be the maintenance of order and the security of those within. This is as it should be. However, what happens to Bartimaeus and the Canaanite woman? Are they left to wander outside the church in their brokenness? Aren't these the "least ones" that Jesus calls us to feed and clothe and welcome?(Matthew 25:31-46) How can the needs of "the least" be reconciled with the comfort and security of the parishioners?

There are two ways in which such reconciliation can be accomplished. First, hospitality must be perceived as ministry among the members of the community not to the members of the community. The service to one's brothers and sisters that engenders a "we/they" attitude is patronizing and harmful and certainly not conducive to building the Kingdom of God. In Matthew's Gospel Jesus identified not with the sheep on the right nor the goats on the left but with the poor, needy, and helpless. A training for hospitality ministers must gently and persuasively, through the experience of its participants, deal with this issue.

Secondly, hospitality does not begin with guidelines and rules for implementing the ministry. It begins at the heart of the

10

matter, with "a spirit, a consciousness, an awareness. With that spirit, techniques are indispensable and highly useful. Without that spirit, techniques are dangerous."[28]

The posture of hospitality, the way our actions reflect the attitude of our hearts, is more important than the rules of hospitality. The Pharisees are consumed with concern about rules; Jesus is not. The method used for catechesis for the ministry of hospitality, therefore, flows both from the belief that a spirit of hospitality is manifested as ministry among all the people of God, especially the least, and that an attitude of hospitality must be internalized before rules and guidelines can be considered.

THE FOUR TASKS OF CATECHESIS

Each of the four sessions will incorporate the four tasks of catechesis: building community, reflecting on stories and beliefs, serving others and praying together.[29] The first task, building community, will be accomplished as the participants experience the unity that is generated as people gather. The theme of oneness in Christ is developed throughout the sessions as the community gathers, learns, serves and prays. It is hoped, after experiencing the effects of gathering and forming community, that the participants, without explanation, will assimilate the value of a community gathered in order to pray.

Community is also built when people meet at a refreshment table. Sharing food at table, a natural human experience, was the center of Jesus' ministry for good reason. Table fellowship provides nourishment that is physical, social and spiritual. Therefore, each session will be preceded by and concluded with an opportunity to share refreshments.

The content or message of the sessions flows from the participants' articulation of their faith stories. As they share their life experiences with partners in small groups or in the larger group, and relate them to the church's stories and teachings, they begin to experience a sense of identity and relationship with each other and with Christ. Derived from the methodology of the Rite of Christian Initiation of Adults, this guiding principle can be described in these words: "Walking with comes before making statements about."[30] Listening to each other's stories and interpreting them through the church's stories as they sit together or walk up and down the aisles of the church, forms a bond of recognition and compassion between parishioners of all ages that would not otherwise be possible. When a community shares its life of faith, the work of hospitality has begun.

Built into every session is the call to service which is the responsibility of every person and community baptized into Christ. The gathering of new ministers has occurred precisely because the call to ministry has been heeded, because God has called and the faithful have responded.

Throughout the sessions, the participants become more and more aware of their baptismal heritage, their call to "put on Christ," their call to witness Christ in the world, their call to serve. Rita Claire Dorner states that

> The catechetical task of praying together is accomplished when symbolic actions are experienced in community: The catechetical process takes into consideration the symbolic actions of the Christian community on the human, biblical and liturgical levels. The process involves a stimulation of memory, imagination and intellect through such symbolic actions as signing with holy water, laying on of hands, sharing bread and wine and especially assembling.[31]

When those who gather are invited to pray with and for each other and the needs of the community, when they are encouraged to share gestures of compassion, and when they are given opportunities to be loving and kind through their prayer experience, they can gradually change the way they think and behave.[32] The prayer experiences, therefore, embody the meaning of each session through: 1) symbolic action, 2) intercessory prayer, 3) praying the Our Father and 4) exchanging the sign of peace. Participants will be encouraged to offer each gesture as "a direct and very clearly intended offer of the love, peace, reconciliation of Jesus and the person to one another. . ."[33]

FORMAT OF THE SESSIONS

Henri Nouwen expands on the necessity of a process of self-emptying rather than acquiring "tools of the trade" for the ministry of hospitality. He points out that "the main problem of service is to be the way without being 'in the way'."[34] This requires a training or process that encourages good will more than skill. Nouwen continues:

> And if there are any tools, techniques and skills to be learned they are primarily to plow the field, to cut the weeds and to clip the branches, that is, to take away the obstacles for real growth and development.[35]

A practical way in which to "plow the field" and prepare ministers "to be the way without being 'in the way'" is to provide the experience of being hospitable. Each catechetical process will offer opportunities for participants to minister to others through hospitality. When participants come to the first session, they will be welcomed by a core group composed of four or five people contacted in advance.

This core group will come early to set up refreshments, arrange seating and prepare the environment. The core group will model hospitality as people arrive, greeting them and inviting them to help themselves to refreshments. Their primary task is to be present to people as they arrive, ready to welcome them in an unhurried, fully attentive manner. At the end of the first session participants will sign up for subsequent core groups. By the end of the four sessions, everyone will have experienced hospitality in very practical terms, both as those who offer it and those who receive it.

The structure of the catechetical process, consisting of four sessions, resembles the four major actions of the Mass: gathering, listening, sharing and going forth. Each of these actions provides a theme for one session. However, every session is a model of Sunday worship in that all of the actions are evident: the community gathers, greets, welcomes; they listen to each other and God's word; they share who they are; they are sent out with a sense of mission, of living the Gospel message.

The liturgical catechesis suggested above is strengthened when attention is given to transitions, both within the sessions and at the beginning and ending of each session. Hospitality is very much a ministry of transition, of moving people from one set of circumstances to the next: from the parking lot to their pews, from thinking "I" to thinking "we," from distraction and confusion to peace and purpose. The sessions, therefore, should reflect this aspect of the ministry. The catechesis concentrates on "making connections" for the participants. For example, when an understanding of the meaning of hospitality in our homes is discussed, a connection can be drawn to the hospitality experienced during the gathering of the assembly. Or, when one is able to express feelings of loneliness and isolation, then a connection can be made to those who, like Bartimaeus or the Canaanite woman or people from the soup kitchen, come to the church seeking welcome.

Hospitality is concerned with beginnings and endings, with saying "hello" and saying "good-bye." The importance of beginnings and endings is understood by playwrights. Guided by the principle that the end of the play is contained in the beginning, a good playwright, who is also a good storyteller, knows better than to cheat the audience with an ending that was not hinted at in the first scenes of the play. It is very much like the mystagogical experiences of neophytes who, having experienced the sacraments of initiation, reflect on those experiences, draw connections perhaps to the early days of their catechumenate and say, "Aha!" Liturgical catechesis must promote the "Aha!" factor. In looking back to the beginning of the process, the participants, through reflection on their experience, can say, "Now I see. Now I understand what hospitality is all about." They will depart with a lived experience of hospitality, just as the assembly is sent out from Sunday worship with a lived experience of faith in community. The seeds of both will have been sown in the gathering rites, the end contained in the beginning.

GROUNDWORK FOR INITIATING THE MINISTRY OF HOSPITALITY

The promotion of the ministry of hospitality proceeds on the basis of at least these two factors: first, support and input from the pastor and liturgist about the needs and characteristics of the parish, and second, considerations about what encourages people to participate in volunteer "educational" activities.

In the pilot program from which this process developed, the pastor expressed a special concern about the long-time, loyal ushers and how they would be incorporated in the program. Heeding that concern, both the pastor and the liturgist prepared a memorandum to all liturgical ministers. This memorandum expressed appreciation for their years of dedicated service and invited them to participate in the sessions.

Announcements were placed for several weeks in the church bulletin, and one appeared in the school bulletin. Eight days before the first session was to begin, seven hundred flyers were inserted into the bulletins. That same day a presentation, preceded by the Presider's introduction, was given at each of the Masses. The priests of the parish had each received a letter verifying the pastor's permission, requesting their support and providing a suggested text for the introduction. All were happy to comply and were very supportive.

In addition to all of the above, personal invitations were extended to prayer groups, liturgical ministers, friends, and those who had expressed interest in the past. An executive of the North American Forum on the RCIA once suggested that sponsors should come "from the middle section of the church," the people who are never asked to do anything.[36] These people were invited. Also invited were those whose enjoyment of people, as expressed through their social skills, was obvious.

Studies suggest that educational programs with certain qualities are more attractive and invitational to adults. Parishioners respond to programs clearly focused on a goal which the participants themselves wish to achieve. They respond to a participatory environment in which their ideas and experiences are valued. They want to gain a better understanding of their role as a minister.

They want a positive experience of fellowships and community and an opportunity to grow in faith.[37]

James DeBoy provided valuable insights into the factors most conducive to adult learning. He wrote that adults learn best when they are

> treated with respect; . . . when the learning selection is related to their past experiences. . . . Adults learn best when they are physically comfortable and can socialize with those in the learning group. . . . (They learn best when there are opportunities for a variety of learning activities; . . . in a problem-centered situation, when a question needs resolution or when a task needs doing; . . . when they can see progress, immediate results and some rewards for the time they put into learning).[38]

CONCLUSION

Based on these studies, several decisions were made. First of all, in consideration of the pastor's desire to encompass all groups in the parish, the sessions were to be open to everyone. Parishioners were encouraged to "meet and share your faith with fellow parishioners, learn about liturgy, develop your hospitality skills and make a difference in your parish." It was hoped this broad appeal to "make hospitality your special care" (Romans 12:13), would attract those who had not found a place for themselves in the parish community.

Second, we made the decision to offer each session twice, once in the evening and once in the afternoon. We hoped the accommodation to the needs of older parishioners and to the availability of working people, would encourage greater participation.

Third, the sessions would be conducted in the gathering area of the church where participants could begin to feel "at home" and comfortable in their place of worship. The arrangement of chairs in a circle would provide better eye contact and a sense of community. Most of all, the participants could begin to claim the "gathering and scattering" area as their own, the place where their ministry is most visibly related to liturgy.

Fourth, the participants would be asked to begin thinking of practical applications of the ministry to the needs of the parish. As emphasized earlier, the development of a spirit of hospitality is more important than designing rules. However, adults needing to see "immediate results for the time they are putting into learning" would appreciate the invitation to begin making a few practical connections in the form of an "idea list" to which they can offer suggestions for hospitality. Each session, therefore, would give participants the opportunity to reflect not only on why but how they would serve, especially during the last session when small groups would "brainstorm" on particular actions of the ministry at the parish. The pastoral dimensions of the ministry, however, would be attended to in greater depth in follow-up sessions or regular meetings of the hospitality ministers.

Finally, a commissioning rite was planned as a conclusion to the process. The pastor and liturgist concurred that it should take place at each of the liturgies on one Sunday. The new ministers of hospitality would be invited to participate at the Mass they normally attended and be prepared to take their places at the doors of the church before and after Mass. The commissioning would be experienced by both the community and the ministers as a sign of their willingness and readiness to serve. An outline of this rite is included in the Appendix.

THREE

The Catechetical Sessions

INTRODUCTION

The methodology for a process of liturgical catechesis for the ministry of hospitality is based on several assumptions. First of all, it is assumed that everyone in the assembly is a minister of hospitality, especially the liturgical ministers: eucharistic ministers, lectors, musicians, ushers, greeters, and altar servers. The ministry, in other words, is not confined to a few people standing at the door greeting parishioners. It extends into the pews, the choir loft and the sanctuary. It is the most human and most demanding of any act of service, for it calls one to become present to every other person, stranger or friend with whom he or she comes into contact.

A second assumption is that we are all called to ministry through our baptism in Christ: Having entered the "water bath" of Jesus, "we die to ourselves, die to merely being individuals and put on Christ, so that we went into the tomb with Christ and we rose with Him. . . . Through baptism, we were grafted onto Christ . . . and onto each other."[39] The joy of the ministry is responding to the Gospel message to love even strangers and those who persecute us; the joy is answering the call of baptism.

A final assumption is that the reality of baptism brings us to the Table of the Lord where we celebrate our unity in Christ. The spiritual nourishment received from the Eucharist and the realization that all who receive it are the Body of Christ, strengthens ministers for the tasks to which they have been called.

These basic assumptions, integral to the formation process, provide direction and shape to the following goals for a ministry of hospitality:

To enable participants to experience the strength of shared faith in community.

To help participants, as they reflect on their stories and beliefs, to draw relationships between what they experience in liturgy and what they experience in life.

To guide participants to recognize their call to service as the privilege and responsibility of their baptism in Christ.

To give participants the opportunity to pray together, to experience themselves as the incarnate Church as they express their humanity through the divine dimensions of their worship together.

These goals, and the assumptions which shape them, provide the outline for each of the four sessions which comprise the catechetical process. The sessions will encourage the growth of hospitality throughout the parish.

SESSION ONE: GATHERING

Catechist's Background

The underlying theology of the session on Gathering is the intimate relationship between liturgy and life. Parishioners who come to this first catechesis for ministers of hospitality will undoubtedly anticipate a "how to" approach: how to greet others warmly, how to seat people without disturbing others, how to help the liturgy run smoothly without distractions. However, these practicalities will be addressed not as a set of guidelines and regulations, but as they relate to the participants' experience of hospitality as an attitude.

The catechetical session, therefore, introduces an unexpected element: it brings those who wish to be ministers of hospitality into the church where they may be surprised to find refreshments available in the vestibule. They will also find chairs set up in a circle in the gathering are or wherever there is space in the church. They will be asked to share their stories, both sad and joyful, so that there may be the sound of conversation and laughter, perhaps unfamiliar in their place of worship. They will be asked to move around the church as they bless one another in those areas that have special meaning for parishioners when they gather for worship. They will reach out to each other as they pray, experiencing themselves as the incarnate church. The link between liturgy and their lives will be more than merely considered; it will be lived. "For the incarnate church . . . is a meeting of real people who speak to and touch each other. In that speaking and touching in Christ's name, the church happens."[40]

The activities and prayers of this first gathering of hospitality ministers will reflect the stories of their families. It is hoped that they will begin to perceive connections between how they interact at home with families and guests and how they interact at church with acquaintances and strangers. Out of their shared reflections should grow an awareness of Church as a place where their lives are celebrated in community. As ministers of hospitality, they must come to believe that "the service they render is for the life of the community, not for the smoothness of the liturgy or the propriety of the assembly."[41]

It is essential at this first session that participants grasp a concept of service as ministry *among* the members of the community, not *to* the members of the community. They should begin to see hospitality as a ministry of the whole assembly, not only as the specific task of a minister who acts as leaven within the community, modeling an attitude of welcome. For the reason, a group of four or five participants will have been invited to help prepare for the session. These novice ministers will begin to experience hospitality in a pastoral way as they model a welcoming attitude. At the same time, those arriving will have an opportunity to respond to the welcome they receive.

It is also important that participants perceive their ministry as a vocation, a "calling from God" within the Church. They need to understand that baptism calls each of us to share in Jesus' vocation of priest, prophet and king (*Decree on the Apostolate of*

Lay People, No. 3). They are called to this time and place by virtue of their baptism; they are called to the ministry of hospitality through their relationship to Christ and the Church as they celebrate this relationship in liturgy and in life.

Integral to this first catechetical session for hospitality ministers is an understanding of the function of the gathering rites within the liturgy. The *General Instruction of the Roman Missal* makes clear that the liturgical assembly itself is a real presence of Christ (GIRM, 7). The gathering rites, therefore, "call the assembly to an awareness of that presence of Christ in its midst."[42] Such awareness influences the attitude and behavior of those who gather and those who minister among the gathered. It is, in fact, the people who minister during the gathering rites "who can make the difference."[43]

Hospitality, then, is approached not as a matter of simply shaking hands, smiling with sincerity and taking people to their places. The ministers who "make the difference" understand that the gathering rites reflect Christ's presence as they bring together many individuals into one community at prayer. According to Joseph Cardinal Bernardin, the gathering time also "means recollecting ourselves personally – not by leaving behind the cares and distractions of home and work, but by bringing them into the light of the gospel."[44] Ministers of hospitality invite the assembly to feel at home in their church so they can comfortably recollect themselves.

Those who are called to this ministry recognize baptism as the source of that call and understand worship as a human experience. Aware of Christ's presence when "two or three gather together," the new ministers will undoubtedly make a difference in the life of the gathered community as they make room for them in their hearts.

Objectives for Session One

To create an environment of warmth and welcome in which participants will begin to feel "at home" in their church

To build community through faith-sharing

To build community through fellowship

To develop an appreciation for the place of hospitality both in the home and in church

To develop an understanding of the function of the gathering rites in liturgy

To experience the action of gathering as a reflection of Sunday worship

To describe the ministry of hospitality and the distinction between ushering and greeting

To communicate appreciation for the service of those who have been ushers

To provide a scriptural basis for the ministry of hospitality

To promote the ministerial role of the assembly in the gathering rites

To help participants see themselves as giving service through the ministry of hospitality

To develop a sense of hospitality as an attitude rather than a set of rules

To begin to consider guidelines which flow from this attitude

To provide practical experience and models of the ministry of hospitality through the formation of core groups for each session

To give participants an opportunity to pray together as they bless each other in their church home.

Preparation for Session One

Prior to the session, the leader will invite a group of people to arrive early and help with preparation. This core group will be given petitions to read for the closing prayer of the session. They will set up refreshments in an attractive manner in the vestibule and arrange chairs in a circle in the gathering area or wherever space allows in the church. This area will be prepared as follows:

1. a table placed in the center of the circle of chairs;
2. a lighted candle on the table;
3. a glass bowl filled with water;
4. a plant, flowers or banner to enhance the gathering area;
5. taped music playing as people arrive.

The core group will welcome participants as they arrive, invite them to help themselves to refreshments and ask them to fill out a name tag and an information card containing the following: name, address, number of years in the parish and ministries in which they are or have been involved.

Materials Needed for Session One

name tags

information cards

pencils or pens

newsprint pad and markers

easel

petitions for the core group to read

The Bible (*The Jerusalem Bible* is used here)

tape recorder and tapes, including "Gather Us In" by Marty Haugen (*Come and Journey*, G.I.A. Publications, Inc. 1985)

song book or one copy of "Gather Us In"

core group sign-up sheet for subsequent sessions

camera and film (candid pictures of participants taken during the refreshment period and the closing prayer will be displayed at the final session)

flowers, plants and/or banner

candle

a glass bowl filled with water

refreshments

Process for Session One

Introduction:

The leader invites everyone to be seated and welcomes them to the first session. Participants are asked to introduce themselves to someone sitting near them whom they do not know well. They might learn something about each other's families, birthplaces, how long they have been a member of the parish. Partners introduce each other to the whole group. [Five minutes]

Opening Prayer:

Leader: Now that we know each other somewhat better, let us pray as a community gathered in Christ's name:

> Loving God, you have called us together to minister to the needs of our parish in a special way. You have asked us to open our hearts to the stranger, to the lonely, the poor and unloved. Help us to recognize and dispel the fears that prevent us from touching the Christ in others. Jesus said, "Where two or three are gathered in my name, there am I in their midst." Help us to reach out in love, trusting that Christ is present in this gathering. We ask this in Jesus' name and through the power of the Holy Spirit. Amen.

Life Experience: What is Hospitality?

With the large group, the leader initiates a discussion using the following questions:

> In your home, how do you make your family feel comfortable?
>
> What is it that makes your children want to come home?
>
> How do you make guests comfortable? Why would they return?
>
> What makes our church a place where people feel comfortable and welcomed?

As insights are shared, they are written on newsprint pad. [The ideas offered at sessions one, two and three will be collated and distributed for consideration at the final session.] When it is appropriate in relation to responses, explain briefly the distinction between ushering and greeting:

> Leader:
>
> All members of the assembly make up a welcoming community and can, therefore, be considered "greeters." Greeters make everyone who comes to worship feel welcome and at home, not only strangers but the parish family as well. They facilitate the kind of welcome and comfort noted on the newsprint pad. The term "usher" refers to those who perform certain duties within the ministry of hospitality such as seating people, providing security and comfort and taking up the collections.

The leader recognizes and expresses appreciation to those who have been ushers in the past.

Faith Reflection:

The leader continues to reflect with the group, making connections between life experiences and scripture.

> Leader:
>
> Hospitality is not a new idea. It is basic to both the teachings of the Hebrew scriptures and the New Testament. [The

leader reads Genesis 18:1-8, briefly pointing out similarities between the text and the responses listed on newsprint.] This story of Old Testament hospitality is typical of the kind of welcome extended to strangers in Mideastern countries even today. Water is scarce; therefore it is precious. The one who offers water, offers life.

The leader reads and shares key phrases of Romans 12: 9-21 from The Jerusalem Bible, connecting them to responses on newsprint pad.

Leader:

Reflect silently on each of the following phrases, asking, "What are these words saying, to us and to our community?"

". . . make hospitality your special care."

"Bless those who persecute you . . . "

"Rejoice with those who rejoice and be sad with those in

sorrow."

How can the advice of Paul be translated into the particular circumstances and needs of our parish? [Responses are recorded on newsprint pad.]

Shared Reflection:

Leader:

Donna Hansen, speaking to the Holy Father during his 1987 visit, asked him to "walk with me." Before you can reach out to others, you need to know individuals and even yourself better as you share your stories of faith.

The leader gives the following directions:

1. Count off so that everyone has a partner. (If there are twenty in the group, count off to ten.) Partners will find a quiet place in the church to talk with one another.

2. You will share why you are here, how you see yourselves making a difference through ministry. Listen carefully

to each other, so you can share the central thought of your partner's story.

3. When your number is called, meet your partner at the table in the center of the circle and sign yourself with holy water, the sign of your baptism, the source of your call to ministry.

[Suggested time: ten minutes]

The leader calls the people together and introduces group discussion.

Leader:

You had a brief opportunity to walk or sit quietly with someone you may not have known very well. Your shared reflections on ministry, the call to service in the Church, are important to us all. Please share, if you are comfortable doing so, one thought or new idea that your partner expressed.

The leader draws connections between their reflections and the responses listed on the newsprint. If there are new thoughts, those are added to the list. The leader requests one-word descriptions of their "walking and sharing" experience and adds those words to the newsprint pad. The leader points out examples of hospitality that have been articulated: closeness, caring, sincerity, respect, compassion, etc. The leader points out that postures of listening and sharing constitute an expression of hospitality. The leader concludes:

"Where two or three are gathered in my name, there am I in their midst." – Matthew 18:20

Closing Prayer (begins in the gathering area)

A Prayer of Blessing for our Church.

The leader begins:

This is our house, and it is natural and right for us to ask for God's blessings on our home and the people in it. Our closing prayer service will take us to areas of the church that have special meaning for us as a worshiping community. We will be hearing the song "Gather Us In" as we pray.

The leader reads the first verse of the song:

> Here in this place, new light is streaming;
> Now is the darkness vanished away.
> See in this space, our fears and our dreamings,
> Brought here to you in the light of this day.
> Gather us in, the lost and forsaken;
> Gather us in, the blind and the lame.
> Call to us now, and we shall awaken;
> We shall arise at the sound of our name.

The leader motions to the participants to rise. The first petition will be read by the leader and the remainder by members of the core group. Background music: "Gather Us In" by Marty Haugen, is played quietly in the background.

> Leader:
>
> You are invited to raise your hands in blessing as you pray.
>
> (In the gathering area)
>
> LOVING GOD, we ask you to pour out your blessings on us as we gather in our parish church. Bless us in this place where we gather and greet one another, where we say say good-bye and are sent forth in love and friendship. We ask this as we raise our hands in blessing. For this, let us pray to the Lord.
>
> RESPONSE: Lord, hear our prayer.
>
> (The participants process to the Reconciliation Room)

After they reach the Reconciliation Room a member of the core group prays:

> LOVING GOD, we ask you to pour out your blessings on the Reconciliation Room; bless us in the place where we receive forgiveness of our sins and healing of our brokenness For this, let us pray to the Lord.
>
> RESPONSE: Lord, hear our prayer.

The participants process to the Blessed Sacrament Chapel or Tabernacle.

> CORE MEMBER: LOVING GOD, pour out your blessings on those who find in the Eucharist a source of life and strength for their journey of faith. For this, let us pray to the Lord.
>
> RESPONSE: Lord, hear our prayer.
>
> (In the sacristy)
>
> CORE MEMBER: LOVING GOD, pour out your blessings on those who prepare for worship here in the sacristy. May all who prepare for worship here truly lead us to reverence you. For this, let us pray to the Lord.
>
> RESPONSE: Lord, hear our prayer.
>
> (Encircling the ambo)
>
> CORE MEMBER: LOVING GOD, pour out your blessings on those who proclaim your Word at the ambo; may it truly be the Table of your Word, and may we be open to and nourished by the Word we hear proclaimed. For this, let us pray to the Lord.
>
> RESPONSE: Lord, hear our prayer.
>
> (Around the altar)
>
> CORE MEMBER: LOVING GOD, pour out your blessings upon those who come to the Table of the Lord, the place where we break and share bread and wine. May the altar always remind us of Christ and call us to worship as one body in Him. For this, let us pray to the Lord.
>
> RESPONSE: Lord, hear our prayer.
>
> (Around the baptismal font)
>
> CORE MEMBER: LOVING GOD, pour out your blessings on those seeking new life at the baptismal font; may all who are baptized here die to self and rise to new life in Christ, we pray to the Lord.
>
> RESPONSE: Lord, hear our prayer.

The leader invites everyone to raise their hands in blessing over each other:

LOVING GOD, pour out your blessings on us, your ministers. Pour out your blessings on the people we serve, those who gather to worship you and to be made holy by you. Pour out your blessings on this, our parish home. May it truly be a home to all who enter here, a sadness to all who depart, a refuge to all who are lost, and a promise to all who believe. (adapted from *Share the Word*, Vol. 7, No. 6)

The leader invites the group to join hands and pray for the needs of the community and then to pray the "Our Father."

The leader concludes:

Earlier we blessed ourselves with holy water, a reminder of the baptism that calls us to that holiness and priesthood we share with Christ, a reminder of our call to serve. We heard the word of God through the Old Testament calling us to offer the water of life to strangers. We heard St. Paul asking us to "make hospitality our special care," and we shared our own needs for love and welcome. Let us conclude our prayer, then, with our partners, making the sign of the cross on each other's foreheads with water from the baptismal font, looking at one another as we say,

"Loving God, I ask you to bless . . . [name]. . . , in the name of the Father and of the Son and of the Holy Spirit. Amen."

When all have done so, the leader invites everyone to exchange a sign of peace:

Let us offer a sign of peace as we go forth to share the Lord's love and witness to His truth.

The leader invites participants to sign up for core groups for the next sessions as they gather for refreshments in the vestibule.

SESSION TWO: LISTENING

Catechist's Background

". . . my word shall not return to me void, but shall do my will, achieving the end for which I send it" (Isaiah 55:11). If the people gathering together in an attitude of welcome could be imaged by soil, then the action of listening to God's word might be compared to the receiving the seed. Received in an environment of warmth and welcome, the word transforms the People of God, making them "fertile and fruitful." "God wants his word to be received attentively and to produce some effect in us."[45] God wants us to *listen.* Psalm 95 cautions: "If today you hear God's voice, harden not your hearts."

The first step, then, in hearing God's word is hospitality, welcoming the word and being *present* to the word in an attitude of openness and acceptance. The *General Instruction of the Roman Missal* states that the purpose of the gathering rites is, in fact, "to make the assembled people a unified community and to prepare them properly to listen to God's word and celebrate the Eucharist." (GIRM, 24)

This second session focuses on Christ's presence in the reading of the word (CSL, 7) and the people present *to* the word. Just as the assembly must be at home in its place of worship, so, too, the assembly should be at home with God's Word. In sharing its stories of faith, the assembly listens and grows in faith. The Introduction to the *Lectionary for Mass* makes clear that the ministry of the word is the task of the entire assembly. The work of the Spirit inspires the gathered people "to a 'hearing' of the word in the full sense, not just in the moment of liturgical celebration but in the whole of life."[46]

What is important here, as Ralph Keifer points out, is that the worshiping community actually has a life on which to reflect and that the church "so lives and acts as to make that life possible."[47]

The *General Introduction* is pointing to the fact that the Scriptures read in church do more than touch our daily lives; they have the power to transform our lives, not simply as individuals but as a community.[48] The disciples on the road to Emmaus, for example, were transformed in their recognition of Jesus "in the breaking of the bread" (Luke 24:3-35). What must not be overlooked is that they had reason, first of all, to break bread together.[49] This communal sharing of story and tradition is the essence of hospitality.

In his *Pastoral Letter on the Liturgy*, Joseph Cardinal Bernardin discusses our common story in terms of active listening. He writes that listening is *not passive* but something we actively *do:* "In the liturgy we are schooled in the art of listening. What we do here, we are to do with our lives – be good listeners to one another, to the Lord, to the world with all its needs.[50] Good listening, Bernardin continues, involves gestures of welcome and postures of acceptance and readiness. Listening involves our entire bodies, minds and hearts. It is being present to the word as the word is present to us and then *acting* upon that word. As Jesus declared, "My mother and my brothers are those who hear the word of God and put it into practice"(Luke 8:21). The community listening at liturgy, therefore, is brought into a bond of communication with the proclaimer when eyes are on the lector, not on the pages of a worship book. Both the proclaimer's and listener's preparation at home – reading, reflecting and *living* with Sunday's word – also enhances that bond.[51]

When the word is proclaimed and received in an attitude of acceptance and readiness, the movement of the assembly from the table of God's word to the table of Christ's body is truly experienced as "one single act of worship."(GIRM, 8) It is experienced, through those who proclaim and those who listen well, as "the dying and rising of Jesus."[52] In the action of the liturgical celebration, "this great work wherein God is perfectly glorified and the recipients made holy," (CSL, 7) the word serves to nourish, instruct, and inspire. Alive with the power of God's spirit, the word commits the assembly and the whole church to the work of the word: "to laboring with [the word] as it turns over the waiting soil, working, irrigating, enlightening, warming it, and furthering its growth."[53]

The word shall do God's will, achieving the end for which God sent it. It shall not return to God void.

Objectives for Session Two

To encourage participants to begin practicing hospitality whenever they gather for worship

To encourage an awareness of active listening – being present to another – as an act of service within the community

To develop an appreciation and understanding of the word in life and in liturgy

To experience "alive and active" participation during the Liturgy of the Word by "walking through" the actions of processing, listening and praying

To determine ways in which ushers can promote attention to the word

To experience the power of the word through communal listening and prayer

To record on newsprint the practical applications of the techniques of hospitality to worship in the parish community

Preparation for Session Two

The core group assigned to this session will arrange chairs in a circle in the gathering area and set up the refreshments in the vestibule. As participants arrive, they welcome them, help find their name tags and invite them to help themselves to refreshments. New participants are asked to fill out an information card. The gathering area is prepared as follows:

1. a table placed in the center of the circle of chairs;
2. a lighted candle on the table;

3. the *Lectionary for Mass,* open to the first reading to be proclaimed during the session;

4. taped music playing as people arrive.

Members of the core group will be asked to prepare petitions and proclaim 2 Timothy 1:6-8. A lector who is participating in the sessions will be prepared to proclaim Isaiah 55:10-11.

Materials Needed for Session Two

name tags

information cards

pencils or pens

newsprint pad, markers and easel

camera

Lectionary for Mass marked for above reading

lighted candle

tape recorder and tape of "Gather Us In" by Marty Haugen (*Come and Journey,* published by G.I.A., 1985)

refreshments

Process for Session Two

Introduction:

The leader invites everyone to be seated and to introduce themselves so that everyone's name, including the newcomers,' will be heard. The core group is introduced and thanked. They are asked to review the first session for the new participants: what one insight or activity is recalled? Others may contribute to this. The leader refers to the list on newsprint from the previous session, adding new ideas if they are mentioned.

Leader:

At the first session we reflected on St. Paul's letter to the Romans, urging them to "make hospitality your special care" (Romans 12:13). Everyone who is participating in these sessions can act with "special care" whenever the community gathers for worship; they do not have to wait for "official designation" to begin ministering.

Opening Prayer:

Leader:

Christ is present in our gathering, as we reach out in "special care" to others, and as we respond to Christ's presence in the word proclaimed. Let us stand, join hands and pray:

Loving God, you have given us life, and you have given us a way in which to celebrate that life. We come together as your holy people in praise and thanksgiving for these gifts. Help us to be open to your word, to listen to your word, to proclaim your word with our lives as we reach out in love to our neighbors. We ask this in the name of your Son, Jesus, and in the power of the Holy Spirit. Amen.

Life Experience: How do we Make Ourselves PRESENT when we Listen?

Leader:

As we discussed and recorded last week, both in our homes and at church, we offer guests or strangers "special care" through attention, respect, sincerity, and so forth. [Referring to list on newsprint] An environment of welcome is created in our homes through the use of music, decor, food and, above all, through stories. As we share our lives through our stories, we and our guests grow in unity and common purpose.

In the larger group, discuss the importance of *active* listening. How can its techniques help us to be *present* to the person who is speaking? Examples from life experiences are encouraged as responses are recorded:

Active listening requires that one be attentive, tuned in and focused on the speaker. One listens without interruption. How do you feel when someone interrupts you when you are speaking? How do you feel when you see eyes wandering to others as you speak?

The listener is present to the moment, not thinking ahead. Do you ever find yourself thinking ahead while listening?

Active listening calls for an openness, an attitude of acceptance, particularly if what is heard is unpleasant or challenging. How do you react when you do not like what you are hearing?

For active listening there must be a willingness to absorb and act on what is heard. Can you offer an example of a time you *acted* on what you heard? When you did not act?

As an *active* process, listening requires asking questions, perhaps re-phrasing what is said to test the accuracy of what was heard. Can anyone give an example of this?

In the large group discuss the sharing of our stories of faith in the Liturgy of the Word, pointing out how active listening as outlined above helps us to be *present* to the Word.

Leader:

In addition to the above, it might help also to image or visualize what is heard during the Liturgy of the Word, to ask ourselves questions which make a connection between what is being said and its meaning for our lives. Can you offer an example of this?

A theologian has said, "A Christian is one who has a Bible in one hand and the newspaper in another."[56] What is this saying to a minister of hospitality? St. Paul, in quite contemporary terms, enjoined the Romans to

"Treat everyone with equal kindness; never be condescending but make real friends with the poor" (Romans 12:16, The Jerusalem Bible).

The leader invites partners to exercise active listening in their sharing of the following question:

Who are "the poor"? and, What does it mean to "make real friends with the poor"?

The leader asks the partners to shape their reflections with the larger group and records key words of the sharing on newsprint. The leader then invites the partners to share a time they felt "left out," lonely or "poor" in the sense of having less to offer, of being less than others.

The group reflects on insights about "the poor," "real friends," and the implications for hospitality ministers. Some possible responses [recorded on newsprint]:

be aware of needs of those who gather for worship

be sensitive to their "poverty," loneliness, isolation or need to be alone

be willing to listen and not judge

be ready to act if necessary

give strangers/visitors space to be comfortable. . .

[Suggested time for entire exercise: twenty minutes]

Faith Reflection:

The leader summarizes the group's discussion. Then she/he says:

As we experience the words that Paul wrote to the Romans and share our own stories of despair and hope, of compassion and kindness, it is easier for us to understand and appreciate the power and presence of God in His word. Listen to the following story from the Hebrew Scriptures. Try to visualize the scene, putting yourself in the place of one of the two characters.

The leader tells (does not read) the story of Elijah and the widow of Zarephath (1 Kings 17). After a few minutes reflection the leader asks:

Did you identify with Elijah or the widow? Why? Having experienced droughts and water rationing or "lean times" ourselves, it is easier to understand the widow's hesitancy.

What would you have done in her place? What is the central message of this story? What does it say to us about the ministry of hospitality? How would you *act* on this story as a hospitality minister?

The leader then describes how God's Word challenges us to be hospitable.

When we identify with the people and events in scripture and when we make ourselves *present* to that word, we are engaged in communication with God through God's word. It becomes apparent that the ministry of hospitality, which calls for an attitude of openness and a willingness to listen actively, has prepared the ground for the rooting of God's word in our lives through all the ways listed. [Refer to newsprint pad and responses that have been recorded.] What we can see is that making people comfortable, "at home," less lonely, and more involved has made them more *present* to the liturgy, more attentive to the word.

We will consider some specific ways in which to apply the techniques of active listening to the Ministry of Hospitality. We will do so through listening to the word as it is experienced during a Sunday liturgy.

An Experience of the Liturgy of the Word

The leader explains that the Liturgy of the Word will be experienced as we "walk through" the actions of processing, listening and praying. The lector is asked to stand and the participants to form a line behind him/her. The leader informs the group that as they process:

The *Lectionary for Mass* will be raised above the lector's head.

When the group reaches the sanctuary, they form a line facing the altar.

Together, the group will reverence the altar by bowing.

After bowing, the participants will move to the pews in front of the ambo. Any questions before beginning?

The group processes as "Gather Us In" is played on tape. When everyone is seated, the leader introduces the reading:

> As we gather together each week on the Lord's Day, we celebrate our unity, and we seek to deepen our community. Everything we have done so far leads us to this moment when we prepare to receive Christ in his word.

Isaiah 55:10-11 is proclaimed by a minister of the word who has prayerfully prepared the reading. (The lector has been instructed to look directly at the assembly on the words, "The word of the Lord," waiting for the response before reflecting silently on the reading.) After a period of silence, the leader continues:

> In the letter to the Hebrews (Hebrews 4:12) we hear that God's word is "alive and active." That seems to be the message in this reading from Isaiah. God's word is like rain and snow that makes the earth fertile and fruitful, giving seed to the one who sows and bread to the one who eats. How were *we* "alive and active" as we listened to God's word?

How can hospitality ministers help the assembly become alive and active in response to the word? Responses may include the following:

1. Look at the lector and not read from the worship books.

2. Prepare beforehand by reading the Sunday scriptures at home.

3. Make connections with our lives and our community. Ask "What is this saying to me, to this community?" In what way does this word have the power to transform me, the community?

4. Try to image or visualize the reading, placing ourselves within the setting. Ministers of hospitality can help the community become "alive and active" in their response to the word by witnessing to the above through their examples of reverence and attention to the word. In all

of these ways hospitality ministers become leaven in the community.

What can ushers do to promote attention to the word and help the community become more alive and active in their worship?

It is hospitable to leave room for those who might arrive after Mass begins. Therefore, people can be encouraged to sit near the front and in the center of the pews before Mass begins, leaving aisle seats and back pews available for latecomers.

Latecomers can be seated

after the opening prayer (before the first reading),

after the Gospel,

or when the assembly sits for preparation of the gifts.[55]

Latecomers should not be seated during the readings, prayers or reflective periods of silence.

The leader concludes:

The ministers of hospitality, as part of the worshiping community, become its most attentive and responsive participants. As a real act of service among the community, their posture and demeanor during the Liturgy of the Word manifest the words of Samuel: "Speak, Lord, your servant is listening" (1 Samuel 3:11).

Closing Prayer:

The leader invites everyone to encircle the ambo.

When we hear the word of God, shouldn't we be like the disciples on the road to Emmaus who said, after recognizing Jesus, "Were not our hearts burning inside us as he talked to us on the road and explained the scripture to us?"(Luke 24:32) It is from that word burning inside us that we are called to pray for the needs of our community:

The leader pauses and looks at the community before saying, "Let us pray to the Lord."

> Creator God, may the power of your word move nations to listen and respond with compassion to the needs of the poor, let us pray to the Lord.
>
> Response: Lord, hear our prayer.
>
> May our church leaders listen with their hearts and reach out to heal those who are hurting, let us pray to the Lord.
>
> Response: Lord, hear our prayer.
>
> Please add your own intentions.

[Two members of the core group who have prepared petitions offer their prayers. Others follow.]

The leader concludes:

> Loving God, we gather all of these prayers in trust and hope as we pray,
>
> "Our Father. . . "
>
> In our sharing and study, we empower one another to understand better our role as ministers of hospitality within the assembly. As a sign of that empowerment and in gratitude for the gifts each brings to this ministry, place your hands on the shoulders of the person next to you and pray silently that the power of God's word will strengthen that person's ministry.

After a brief silence, a member of the coregroup reads 2 Timothy 1:6-8:

> "I remind you to stir into flame the gift of God bestowed when my hands were laid on you. The Spirit God has given us is no cowardly spirit, but rather one that makes us strong, loving, and wise. Therefore, never be ashamed of your testimony to our Lord, nor of me, a prisoner for his sake; but with the strength which comes from God bear your share of the hardship which the gospel entails."

The leader invites everyone to offer a sign of peace:

Let us exchange a sign of peace as we leave to bring God's word and God's peace into the world.

The leader announces that at the next meeting everyone will receive a list of "hospitality ideas" that have evolved from the sessions. The participants can begin to think of additional ways in which they would like to see the ministry of hospitality function in the parish community.

The leader reminds participants that refreshments are available in the vestibule.

SESSION THREE: SHARING

Catechist's Background

It is essential that those who gather for worship, especially ministers of hospitality who give witness to the community, have an understanding of eucharist as meal. Such an understanding is important for several reasons. First, as Philippe Rouillard reminds us, "In instituting the Eucharist Christ took not only the signs of bread and wine but also the sign of the meal."[56] Second, the meal "implies an idea of communion and sharing: those who share a same meal constitute a same body."[57] Third, sharing a meal is "a medium for celebrating the mystery of Jesus' dying and rising."[58] It is a sacramental action which celebrates transformation in the use of bread and wine. Bread and wine are also symbols of nourishment, human work and human life which reflect the dying and rising cycle of nature. "But these symbols are not objects; they are taken and shared in the setting of a meal so that participants can experience in these signs the life of Christ and the life of grace he offers us."[59]

The eucharist as meal is a tangible act of hospitality. What this means is easier to understand within the context of the family. When families gather at the table, they share their lives as well as food. It is the place where their identity as family is most visibly expressed. When their hospitality is extended to guests, the family grows beyond itself. In the sharing of its meal and its home, the family is sharing everything that makes it a family.

In much the same way, all who come to the Table of the Lord are nourished, made one and, at the same time, realize themselves as Church. They are also made whole and holy. Wholeness and holiness, although often linked, are not the same reality, and hospitality ministers need to perceive the difference. Wholeness is something human beings work to achieve; holiness is a gift from God. Wholeness gives greater freedom to choose holiness.[60] Distinguishing between the two will enable hospitality ministers to minister to human needs (comfort, security, well-being, warmth and welcome) in order to promote wholeness in worship. At the same time ministers of hospitality recognize and respect that spiritual relationship whereby human beings identify with and imitate God. It is that relationship which is named holiness.[61] Both the human and divine elements of worship expressed in the eucharist – wholeness and holiness, nourishment of body and soul, being one with the community and one with Christ – are always in the hospitality minister's conscious awareness.

The document *Environment and Art in Catholic Worship* gives beautiful testimony to the importance of the human and divine aspects of our worship:

> An action like liturgy, therefore, has special significance as a means of relating to God, or responding to God's relating to us. . . . God has graciously loved us on our own terms, in ways corresponding to our condition. Our response must be one of depth and totality, of authenticity, genuineness, and care . . . (EACW, 13)

It is the responsibility of the ministers of hospitality to prepare the way for authentic, genuine and caring response in the celebration of eucharist. To do so, they must cultivate a refined sense of the meal as the focus and essence of eucharistic celebration.

It is difficult to reach this level of awareness in a society where fast, plastic meals are consumed "on the run." Charles Gusmer observed that the understanding of eucharist as meal may be appreciated "in proportion to our ability to share any human meal."[62] The common experience of meal today has seriously impaired its symbolic value. We cannot value what we do not experience, and this has everything to do with celebrating eucharist in a whole and holy fashion. As Tad Guzie writes:

> Until we experience in our own households the holiness
> of a meal shared in Jesus' name, we will not really grasp
> the import and power of the eucharist as it is enacted in
> the great church.[63]

It is time that Christians recover the power of the meal. They need to pause and bless their food and bless God and themselves in their daily lives. As it becomes habit to do so, the gathered assembly, led by the ministers of hospitality, can begin to experience itself as a welcoming and welcomed community, ready to listen to its story in the word, ready to remember its past and give thanks and praise for the wonder of God's presence in their lives as they approach the Table of the Lord.

Objectives for Session Three

> To point to the meal as a sign of God's presence in the
> ordinary events of our daily lives
>
> To appreciate, as hospitality ministers, the power of the
> meal to unify and bring harmony and strength to families and community
>
> To understand hospitality ministers as hosts in promoting "wholeness" in preparation for eucharist: a sense of
> comfort, well-being, warmth and welcome
>
> To instill a sense of responsibility for paving the way to
> an authentic, genuine and caring response in the celebration of eucharist
>
> To gain insights into transformation, and "signs of transformation," as they are experienced in human and liturgical terms

To continue recording practical applications of techniques of hospitality as they arise in discussion

To appreciate the importance of the full and active participation of the assembly in the Eucharistic Prayers as an act of service to the community

To experience the movement of the Liturgy of the Eucharist from the presentation of the gifts through gathering around the Table of the Lord

To gather around the altar and pray for the needs of the community

To experience an agape, a sign of Christian love, in the sharing of bread and wine

To develop an awareness of hospitality and its ministers as signs of Christian love and service in the world

Preparation for Session Three

The core group will arrange chairs in the gathering area and set up the refreshments. As participants arrive, they welcome them and help them find their name tags. New participants are asked to fill out an information card. The core group gives a worship book to people as they enter. One person is asked to prepare Mark 14:22-26 to read during the closing prayer. The gathering area is prepared as follows:

1. a loaf of bread, wine, wheat and grapes placed on a center table;

2. a lighted candle;

3. taped music playing as people arrive.

Materials Needed for Session Three

name tags

information cards

pencils or pens

newsprint pad, markers and easel

symbols for Session Three: a loaf of bread on a plate, wine, wheat and grapes

camera

slide projector, screen and prepared slides and tape

two tape recorders, one in the gathering area and one in the sanctuary

tape of "Gather Us In" by Marty Haugen (*Come and Journey*, G.I.A.)

tape of a communion hymn

Lectionary marked at Mark 14:22-26

handout: list of "hospitality ideas" culled from Sessions One and Two [Included in Appendix]

refreshments (bread and wine or grape juice)

Process for Session Three

Introduction:

Everyone is welcomed, especially new participants who may have joined the gathering. The leader asks for feedback from the last session: what images, actions, or stories are recalled? Important points of Session Two to be remembered:

1. Christ is present in the word. In its proclamation and *in our hearing* of the word, Christ is present, "alive and active."

2. The poor are those who are in need and their need sometimes makes them feel left out, or less worthy. A real friend is sensitive and compassionate to these feelings. (Romans 12:14-19)

As other ideas or insights are recalled, relevant items on the list of "Hospitality Ideas," a compilation of thoughts about initiating the ministry are pointed out. The list will be distributed at the end of the session for further reflection at home.

Opening Prayer:

Leader:

As we consider practical ways in which to incorporate hospitality in our liturgical celebrations, we remember always that Christ is present in our gathering. Everything we do flows from our awareness of His presence.

Creator God, your Son, Jesus, promised that wherever two or three gather in His name, He would be there in our midst. Trusting in this promise, we open our hearts to receive you, to receive your life and action in ourselves, in each other, in your Word, and in the Eucharist. We ask this in the name of Jesus, your Son, and through the power of the Holy Spirit. Amen.

Life Experiences: How and Why is the Experience of Meal Important in our Lives?

The leader divides the participants into groups of three and requests that they share their remembrance of a memorable meal. [about five minutes] Everyone rejoins the larger group. Factors common to a "memorable" meal are discussed. The following points may be included:

1. Meals have a bonding power, the ability to bring diverse people into a unified whole.

2. The meal strengthens the family and strengthens the community as lives are shared.

3. People forgive and are reconciled at meals.

4. Thanksgiving is expressed at meals.

The leader might focus the group's attention on their own and the assembly's action during the Communion Rite. How do they prepare to receive the eucharist? What helps and what takes away from their preparation and composure?

Faith Reflection

The leader explains that we are *participants,* not spectators, in the eucharist. As such we sing and pray the acclamations, joining the presider in his proclamation of praise. It is the responsibility of the ministers of hospitality, as an act of service within the assembly, to lead the way to full and active participation in the eucharistic prayers.

> Leader:
>
> The power of the meal to unify and bring harmony and strength to families and the community is fully experienced in the actions of the eucharist. As we gather for eucharist we become one body; we become holy.

The leader introduces a reflection on eucharist and transformation by calling attention to the symbols on the center table: wheat, bread, grapes, wine. How are these objects seen as "signs of transformation?"

> The leader summarizes the responses:
>
> Bread and wine possess great symbolic value. They are not natural products. They require processing by humans who transform grain into bread and grapes into wine. They are the "fruit of the earth [or vine], work of human hands."[64]
>
> An entire history is contained in the growing of grain: death and resurrection in the earth. (To continue the analogy from Sessions One and Two: if gathering is preparing the soil and listening is planting the seed, then sharing the eucharistic meal is the nourishing of that seed.) Bread is a symbol of work and of life and, "when shared, it is charged with familial and social value."[65] From earliest times, a meal represented an entire day in the life of a family from its production and gathering in the fields to its preparation and consuming at table.

Wine too is a product of care and preparation:

1. Wine gives vigor and vitality; it is regarded as a drink of life and immortality.

2. Wine is "an efficacious symbol of sharing and communion." In the Jewish wedding ritual, for instance, the young couple drinks from the same cup which is then broken as a sign that no third party can be part of their union.[66]

The bread and wine are complementary: bread responds to human hunger, wine to thirst; bread is fruit of the earth, wine fruit of the sun; bread is a material food, wine a spiritual beverage; bread is assimilated and transformed in our bodies, "while the wine has the power to transform," to cause us "to become other."[67]

Closing Prayer:

Leader:

Last week we experienced the power of the word when it is proclaimed and received in an attitude of acceptance and readiness. We move from the table of God's word to the table of Christ's body in "one single act of worship"(GIRM, 8) as the gifts of the people are brought forward to be transformed.

The participants, led by members of the core group, gather behind those carrying the symbols of eucharist and process forward as "Gather Us In" is played. Each person reverences the altar, bowing, and all gather around as the gifts are placed on the altar. Mark 14:22-26 is read by a member of the core group.

Core group member:

The bread which we break is the sign of our unity with God and with one another. Let us pray for the needs of our brothers and sisters in Christ. The response is, "Lord, nourish us."

Spontaneous intercessory prayer modeled by the core group is offered at this time.

Core group members conclude:

You do nourish us, Lord, with the bread of salvation, the wine of hope. With trust we pray the words that Jesus taught us:

"Our Father"

Reflection on Agape (Christian Love) and Eucharist:

Music can be played quietly in the background during the following reflection. A communion hymn would be appropriate.

Leader:

Hospitality is a sign of Christian love. In the early Christian community this Christian love was called *agape*, a Greek word that referred to a love feast or a shared meal. It was not the eucharist. Today Christian communities sometimes celebrate their love with an agape, a sharing of bread and wine. As ministers of hospitality, we are signs of Christian love.

Whenever we share a meal, whether it is in our homes or at the refreshment table in the vestibule or having coffee and doughnuts after Mass, the action of eating together is a sign of that Christian love. It is the love we bring to the Table of the Lord. Hospitality ministers, as liturgical ministers and members of the assembly, must always be aware of their place at that table.

Gathered around the Banquet Table of the Lord, we are never alone. We are sitting with Abraham, Moses, Mary and Joseph. We can be ashamed of our lack of commitment, but we are at table with Archbishop Romero. We might be ashamed of our lack of poverty, but we are at table with Mother Teresa and St. Francis. We might be proud of our education, but we are at table with St. Augustine and St. Jerome. We might be proud of our teaching or preaching, but we are at table with St. Paul. (Adapted from a talk by Rev. J. Nisbet)

In the spirit of all of these saints and good people with whom we touch hands across the world and through time when we gather around the table of the Lord, let us offer a sign of Christ's peace.

Leader: Let us go in peace.

All: thanks be to God.

Conclusion

Copies of "Hospitality Ideas" are distributed (See Appendix B). Participants are encouraged to add ideas to the list for discussion and "brainstorming" at the next and final session. All are invited to enjoy refreshments – *agape!* – in the vestibule.

SESSION FOUR: BEING SENT AND GOING FORTH

Catechist's Background

The analogy of seeds planted and nourished has illustrated the various actions of the liturgy throughout the catechetical process for hospitality ministers. It is in the action of being sent to do Christ's work in the world that the analogy is most appropriate. Hospitality has prepared the ground for those who come together in Christ's name. In the action of listening to God's word at the Table of the Word, the seed of God's will is planted in the lives of those who listen. That seed, nourished and strengthened at the Table of the Eucharist is now sent into the world to blossom and bear fruit.

This final session is about endings; it is about dismissals, blessings and farewells. It must be remembered that everything that happens at the end of the liturgy, like a good story, is contained in the beginning. The end is the beginning. "We are called together in order to be sent forth."[68] Hospitality is that movement of the spirit which points us in the right direction. The dismissal rite acknowledges that in the time between the entrance rite and the final blessing, God has been present to the gathered people in a wonderful and mysterious way. The blessing commissions the assembly to go forth "in peace to love and serve the Lord."[69] The work of hospitality which has begun when the assembly gathers, continues as the assembly scatters. Poised at the thresh-old, the community is prepared to take its blessing into the world. In the words of T.S. Eliot,

> What we call the beginning is often the end
>
> And to make an end is to make a beginning.
>
> The end is where we start from.[70]

Objectives for Session Four

To review the symbolic actions of the first three sessions within the context of hospitality

To give participants an opportunity to share their experiences of saying good-bye, from simple expressions of farewell to more complex and deeply felt expressions

To lead participants to an understanding of the dismissal rite as an act of hospitality

To encourage ministers of hospitality to perceive good-byes as opportunities for blessing

To provide an opportunity for participants to reflect on their past experiences and future directions within the ministry of hospitality

To list and prioritize the hospitality needs of the parish

To perceive the ministry of hospitality as an act of service which extends into the community

To provide an opportunity for participants, within the context of a prayer service, to bless one another for the work they will do as ministers of hospitality.

Preparation for Session Four

The core group assigned to this session will arrange chairs in a circle in the gathering area and prepare the refreshment table in the vestibule. As participants arrive, they welcome them, help them find their name tags and invite them to help themselves to refreshments. One of the core group is prepared to read Luke 10:1-3. The gathering area is prepared as follows:

1. four or five lighted candles and a flowering plant placed on a center table;

2. card tables for four to six people each – set up outside the circle;

3. newsprint and markers at each table;

3. taped music playing as people arrive;

4. bulletin board display of the candid pictures taken during the first three sessions.

Materials Needed for Session Four

name tags

a candle for each participant placed on a table near the baptismal font

four or five card tables depending on number of participants

newsprint and marking pens for each table

masking tape

four or five candles and a flowering plant on center table

tape of "Gather Us In" by Marty Haugen (*Come and Journey*, G.I.A.)

Lectionary marked for Luke 8:1-16

bulletin board display of candid pictures

refreshments

Process for Session Four

Introduction:

The leader thanks the core group, welcomes everyone and invites
the participants to sit with someone they do not know well.

> Leader:

> We have talked about hospitality as an "attitude," a way
> of behaving that reflects our acceptance and love of the
> "stranger in our midst." It is a reaching out, an emptying
> of ourselves to make room for the other. As ministers of
> hospitality, we have begun to see ourselves as . . . [the
> following descriptions are elicited from the group: posi-
> tive, open, willing, supportive, reverent, kind, dependable,
> warm, receptive/accepting, generous, grateful . . .] In sum-
> mary, a minister of hospitality "makes real friends with
> the poor" (Romans 12:16).

The leader reminds the group that we are not passive spectators
when we worship together. An attitude of change is implied
whenever "worship"is perceived as something we *do*. The group
is invited to recall the symbolic actions of our worship together
by reflecting on the symbols of each session:

1. Session One: blessing with water, a sign of baptism and
   call to ministry

2. Session Two: proclaiming God's Word from the *Lectionary*, a sign of God's presence in the Word

3. Session Three: sharing wheat and grapes, bread and
   wine; signs of transformation

> Leader:

> How do these actions become acts of hospitality?

> How do you see yourself acting now that might be different
> from the actions that preceded the raising of your "hospi-
> tality awareness"? [share with partner for about five min-
> utes]

Reflections are shared in the larger group. The following points
may be included:

1. Christ is present whenever two or three gather in His name. Christ is present in the assembly, the minister, the Word, the bread and wine, the sacraments.

2. We come to know each other better when we "walk" together.

3. We empower one another through our blessings and prayers.

4. Whenever Christians gather, they pray for the needs of the community and the whole world.

The leader includes other relevant points from the reflections.

Opening Prayer:

During the last four weeks we have come to know each other in a deeper way through the stories, prayers and blessings we have shared. Let us join hands and pray now for God's blessing on our endeavors as ministers of hospitality:

> Loving God, we have responded to your call to gather in your name. We have gathered, listened, and shared in the name of Jesus. We ask you to bless us now as we move forward in your name to be the "body of Christ" in the world. Help us, as ministers of hospitality, to be the leaven which transforms the world into your Kingdom. We ask this in the name of Jesus, your Son and through the power of the Holy Spirit. Amen.

Life Experience: How do we say Good-bye?

> Leader:
>
> Families have rituals for every part of their lives together. This is most obvious at family celebrations such as birthdays or special dinners. But sometimes the most ordinary actions can become a ritual. Saying good-bye is an example. When our family says good-bye, everyone goes outside and stands on the curb, waving until the person leaving is out of sight. What are some ways your family or friends

say good-bye? [Responses are shared in the large group.] What about special good-byes? Do you remember when a child left for college? Or the first time you or a friend moved away? What about saying good-bye to someone leaving for one or more years? [Responses are shared in the large group.]

Sometimes the separation is indefinite. We do not know if we will ever see the other person, at least in our lifetime. Have you ever experienced that kind of good-bye? Please share with your partners your experience of a memorable farewell, paying attention to both the good and the negative aspects of such a good-bye. [About five minutes]

The leader invites the partners to share in the larger group some of their insights about the profound effects of such farewells, both difficult and transforming. The leader summarizes the sharing and says:

Leader:

The words we use today to indicate leave-taking, point to blessing: *adieu, adios, good-bye* ("God be with ye.") These all "are human well-wishings that commit another person to the care of God."[73]

Faith Reflection:

The leader points out that good-byes are experiences of "dying and rising." Changes are necessary in our lives in order that there can be growth.

Leader:

"I solemnly assure you, unless the grain of wheat falls to the earth and dies, it remains just a grain of wheat. But if it dies, it produces much fruit" (John 12:24).

The Church has always tried, sometimes more successfully than others, to meet human needs; this is especially true of the way it helps people deal with final good-byes. But the Church, in its liturgy, also deals with ordinary good-byes. What we learn from the Church's good-bye is that a good-bye is also a blessing.

1. The roots of such action in the liturgy can be found in Hebrew Scripture where "the act of blessing . . . imparts vital power to another person."[72]

    a. In the Hebrew Scriptures power is imparted when a father blesses his son (Genesis 27). Jacob steals his brother's blessing and receives the family inheritance. The blessing is an indication of the transference of power.

    b. In the Book of Ruth, Naomi bids her widowed daughters-in-law good-bye, asking God's blessings on them. But Ruth refuses to leave her mother-in-law's side and departs for a new land where her act of piety and integrity brings her many more blessings. Ruth's loving response to her mother-in-law's farewell blessing influences the course of history, for she becomes the ancestor of David and Christ.

2. In Christian Scriptures Jesus often blesses his disciples. One example is just before he ascends to the Father:

    Then he led them out near Bethany, and with hands upraised, blessed them. As he blessed, he left them, and was taken up to Heaven (Luke 24:50-51).

3. The concluding rite of the liturgy sends the assembly forth with the priest's blessing, dismissing them "to do good works, praising and blessing the Lord." (GIRM, 57) The assembly is empowered by the Mass to do such work.

    a. The Latin root for the word mass is *missa*. It means "sending" or "mission." In the Latin Mass, the words *"Ite missa est"* implied both the end of the sacred service and a blessing. In the early history of the Church, the term came to be applied to the entire ceremony.

    b. "The entire mass is a blessing, a sanctification."[73]

The leader initiates the dialogue that takes place between the presider and the assembly during the dismissal rite and invites the participants' response.

The priest blesses people:

> "May almighty God bless you, the Father, and the Son, and the Holy Spirit." The people respond: "Amen."

> Then he says or sings one of the following:

> "Go in the peace of Christ." The people respond, "Thanks be to God."

> Or, "The Mass is ended, go in peace." "Thanks be to God."

> "Go in peace to love and serve the Lord." "Thanks be to God."

> We have been blessed and sent forth to "do good works, praising and blessing the Lord." A question to ponder, not now, but later: how are these words translated into acts of hospitality? (In other words, what difference does the blessing and sending forth to "do good works" make in our lives after we leave the church?)

Applications of the Ministry of Hospitality

The leader asks the participants to divide into groups so there are four to six people at each card table. They can carry their own chairs to the table.

1. Referring to the list of "Hospitality Ideas" that was distributed at the last session, each group compiles a list of needs. One person should record the answers.

2. When the list is completed, the items should be prioritized.

3. Chairs are returned to the circle. Each group shares the three highest items on its list with the larger group.

4. The leader will record these items, and the larger group will prioritize this list.

[Projected time for activity: about thirty minutes]

The leader will compile the list, giving copies to the pastor and parish staff and mailing it to everyone who participated in the sessions. A date and time for an organizational meeting is set.

Leader:

Both Martha and Mary in Luke's Gospel are ministers of hospitality (Luke 10:38-42). Mary is present to the Lord, her full attention on Him, and in this way she *energizes* hospitality. Martha is running the kitchen, tending to the dinner. She *engineers* hospitality. Both qualities are necessary in the ministry. As new ministers of hospitality, we have just experienced Martha's task.

Announcements:

The leader reminds the group when it will meet again and announces the date of the commissioning rite which will take place at all of the Sunday liturgies. New ministers of hospitality can participate at the Mass they normally attend and be prepared to take their places at the doors of the church before and after Mass. In order to ascertain the number of ministers at each Mass, the group is asked to sign the sheet available at the refreshment table following the closing prayer.

Closing Prayer:

The core group places the lighted candles from the center table on each card table. Participants are invited to return to their small groups, standing around the card tables.

Leader:

Please listen to the words of the first verse of "Gather Us In" as it is played before processing to the baptismal font. One person from each group can carry the candle.

When all of the groups have surrounded the baptismal font and the candles have been placed on a table nearby, the leader continues:

> We are the "new light" shining. In the grateful spirit of a people gathered in Christ's name, let us listen to the Good News of the Lord.

A member of the core group reads Luke 8:16

> A reading from the Gospel of Luke.
>
> "No one lights a lamp and puts it under a bushel basket or under a bed; he puts it on a lampstand so that whoever comes in can see it."
>
> The Gospel of the Lord.
>
> Leader:
>
> We have walked together on a journey of love with Christ as our light. In confidence and trust, we turn to Christ as we pray for the needs of our community. The response is, "Lord, hear our prayer."

Spontaneous intercessory prayer is offered at this time.

> The leader concludes:
>
> We gather up these needs and offer them to you, Father, as we pray the words that Jesus taught us: "Our Father"
>
> Leader:
>
> Christ told us that "No one lights a lamp and puts it under a bushel basket." We are called to be that light for each other and for the world. During these last weeks together, you have each been a light. Thank you for the concern, the care and attention you have given each other and the new ministry of hospitality. As a sign of the light that you bring into the world, please take a lighted candle home with you.

The leader and core group distribute the candles, the leader lighting the first candle. The light is passed on to the others. When all the candles are lit, the leader continues:

Loving God, pour out your blessings on all who have gathered here. Pour out your blessings on the work that we do. Pour out your blessings on our families and friends, on our parish community and all those in our community we are called to serve.

Go forth with a sign of Christ's love and peace.

Go forth as light into a darkened world.

FOUR

Conclusion

The catechetical process should be understood as open-ended. Renewal sessions can be offered in conjunction with a retreat day or evening for all of the liturgical ministries. All ministry requires constant revitalization through catechesis, affirmation and the periodic withdrawal from the world provided by such retreats.

As the vital role of hospitality in the celebration of liturgy is understood and appreciated more deeply by liturgical ministers and the assembly, it is hoped that more parishioners will be moved to take an active part in the ministry. Above all, it is hoped that the spirit of hospitality will pervade the community in such a way that there really is no distinction between host and guest at the parish.

Summary

We began with reference to the early Christian community and the importance of gathering and becoming one. It seems appropriate to conclude with the impassioned words of a third century document on church life:

> . . . command and exhort the people to be faithful to the assembly of the church. Let them not fail to attend, but let them gather faithfully together. Let no one deprive the Church by staying away; if they do, they deprive the body of Christ of one of its members!
>
> For you must not think only of others but of yourself as well, when you hear the words that our Lord spoke: "Who

does not gather with me, scatters" (Mt. 12:30). Since you
are the members of Christ, you must not scatter yourselves
outside the Church by failing to assembly there.[74]

The task of hospitality is to facilitate the gathering of the
Christian community. Hospitality ministers are called to make
space within the community for all who are called to worship.
They are called to create an environment of warmth and welcome
in which people can become whole and holy. Hospitality ministers
are also called to make space within themselves for the other.
They are called to embrace indiscriminately and love wholeheart-
edly.

People will not stay away when they learn they have been
missed, when they know that their presence makes a difference
and that the celebration is not the same without them. To evoke
this kind of response and to make this kind of difference in a
parish is an art, the art of hospitality. It ensures that the Church
will not be deprived of any of its members:

> . . . so let your Church be gathered
> from the ends of the earth into your kingdom,
> for yours is glory and power through all ages

Endnotes

1. "The Didache," text from Lucien Deiss, *Springtime of the Liturgy*, trans. Matthew O'Connell (Collegeville: The Liturgical Press, 1979), 75.
2. *The Sacramentary*, trans. ICEL (New York: Catholic Book Publishing Co., 1985), 552.
3. Joseph Gelineau, *Learning to Celebrate* (Washington, D.C.: The Pastoral Press, 1985), 5.
4. Kenneth Smits, "A Congregational Order of Worship," *Living Bread, Saving Cup*, ed. R. Kevin Seasoltz (Collegeville: The Liturgical Press, 1982), 284.
5. *Ibid.*, 286.
6. David N. Power, *Gifts that Differ: Lay Ministries Established and Unestablished* (New York: Pueblo Publishing Company, 1980), 156.
7. *Constitution on the Sacred Liturgy*, No. 14.
8. Eugene Walsh, S.S.: "Hospitality: Heartbeat of Participation," *Modern Liturgy* 12 (March 1985): 5.
9. Karl Rahner, "The Theology of the Symbol," *A Rahner Reader*, ed. Gerald A. McCool (New York: Seabury Press, 1975), 121.
10. Henri J. M. Nouwen, *Reaching Out* (Garden City: Image Books, 1975), 71.
11. *Ibid.*, 66.
12. *Ibid.*
13. *Ibid.*, 67.
14. James Lopresti, "What Kind of Rite does the Church Want?" *North American Forum on the Catechumenate*, Asilomar, California, 22 May 1987.
15. Regina Kuehn, "A Climate of Hospitality," *Liturgy* 80, 13 (April 1982): 8.
16. Nouwen, 107.
17. *Ibid.*, 76-77.

18. Ralph A. Keifer, *To Hear and Proclaim* (Washington, D.C.: National Association of Pastoral Musicians, 1983), 62.
19. *Ibid.*
20. *Ibid.*, 70.
21. *Ibid.*, 71.
22. *Ibid.*, 70
23. James Dallen, *Gathering for Eucharist: A Theology of Sunday Assembly* (Old Hickory, Tennessee: Pastoral Arts Associates of North America, 1983), 38.
24. *Ibid.*, 39.
25. Nouwen, 109.
26. Kuehn, 10.
27. George R. Szews, "Ministers of Hospitality and Greeting," *Liturgy: The Rites of Gathering and Sending Forth 1*, no. 4 (1981): 20.
28. Robert W. Hovda, *Strong, Loving and Wise* (Collegeville: The Liturgical Press, 1985), 1.
29. Anne Marie Mongoven, "The Directory: A Word for the Present." *The Living Light* 16 (Summer 1979): 135-148.
30. James Lopresti, 22 May 1987.
31. Rita Claire Dorner, Class notes, *Liturgical Catechesis*, 23 January 1985, Santa Clara, California.
32. William Cieslak, "Hospitality," *Liturgical Institute*, Diocese of Oakland. Cassette, 1984.
33. Eugene A. Walsh, S.S., *The Order of Mass: Guidelines* (Glendale, Arizona: Pastoral Arts Associates of North America, 1979), 47.
34. Nouwen, 108.
35. *Ibid.*
36. Karen Hinman Powell, "Preparing a Catechumenate Team and Ministries of the RCIA," *North American Forum on the Catechumenate, Asilomar*, California, 18 May 1987.
37. Gloria Durka, Class notes, *Family Ministry*, Summer 1987, Santa Clara University, Santa Clara, California.
38. James J. DeBoy, "Getting Started in Adult Religious Education," (New York: Paulist Press, 1979): 75-78.
39. Cieslak, "Hospitality," Cassette.
40. James F. White, "Coming Together in Christ's Name," *Liturgy: The Rites of Gathering and Sending Forth 1*, no. 4 (1981):7.
41. George R. Szews, 21.
42. Keifer, 70.
43. Szews, 21.

44. Joseph Cardinal Bernardin, *Our Communion, Our Peace, Our Promise: Pastoral Letter on the Liturgy* (Chicago: Liturgy Training Publications, 1984), 7.

45. Francis J. Buckley, *Reconciling* (Notre Dame: Ave Maria Press, 1981), 38.

46. Keifer, 76.

47. *Ibid.*, 77.

48. *Ibid.*

49. *Ibid.*

50. Bernardin, 9-10.

51. *Ibid.*, 11-12.

52. James B. Dunning, *Ministries: Sharing God's Gifts* (Winona: Saint Mary's Press, 1985), 82.

53. Gelineau, *Learning to Celebrate*, 19.

54. Joseph Grassi, Class notes, *Teaching the Word of God*, 30 June 1986, Santa Clara.

55. Gregory F. Smith, O. Carm., *The Ministry of Ushers* (Collegeville: The Liturgical Press, 1980), 22.

56. Philippe Rouillard, "From Human Meal to Christian Eucharist," *Living Bread*, Saving Cup, ed. R. Kevin Seasoltz (Collegeville: The Liturgical Press, 1982), 132.

57. *Ibid.*, 133.

58. Charles Gusmer, "Is the Mass a Meal?" *Catholic Update* (Cincinnati: St. Anthony Messenger Press, 1977), 2.

59. Kevin W. Irwin, Liturgy, *Prayer and Spirituality* (New York: Paulist Press, 1984), 54.

60. Theodore E. Dobson, *Say But The Word: How the Lord's Supper Can Transform Your Life* (New York: Paulist Press, 1984), 8.

61. *Ibid.*

62. Gusmer, 2.

63. Tad Guzie, "Reclaiming the Eucharist," *Liturgy: Central Symbols* 7, no. 1 (1987): 33.

64. Rouillard, 129.

65. *Ibid.*

66. *Ibid.* 130.

67. *Ibid.*, 131. T.S.

68. Marchita Mauck, "Rites at the Closing of a Liturgy," *Liturgy: The Rites of Gathering and Sending Forth 1*, no. 4 (1981):77.

69. Ibid.

70. T.S. Eliot, "Little Gidding," *The Art of T.S. Eliot*, Helen Gardner (New York: E.P. Dutton and Company, 1950), 9.

71. William H. Willimon, "The Peace of God Go with You," *Liturgy: The Rites of Gathering and Sending Forth 1*, no. 4 (1981):67.

72. *Ibid.*, 69.

73. Mauck, 77.

74. "The Didascalia of the Apostles," text from Lucien Deiss, *Springtime of the Liturgy:* 176-7.

APPENDIX A

Commissioning Rite

(This rite was prepared for use during Mass on the Thirty-fourth or last Sunday of the Year, Cycle A. It may be used as a model for commissioning during Mass on other Sundays when the Gospel is appropriate for such a rite.)

COMMISSIONING RITE FOR HOSPITALITY MINISTERS

Presider returns to presidential chair after homily.

COMMENTATOR: Several weeks ago, a number of parishioners participated in a four-week training course for the Ministry of Hospitality. We ask those participants to come forward to receive a blessing for their ministry. And we invite everyone, as members of the assembly, to stretch forth your hands in blessing and to respond "Amen."

Hospitality Ministers, wearing name tags, move to the front and stand at Presider's right.

PRESIDER: [Addressing Hospitality Ministers] Stretches forth his hands and says: In Matthew's Gospel, Jesus says to his disciples: "When the Son of Man comes in his glory: . . . he will say to those on his right, "Come, you who are blessed by my Father. Inherit the kingdom prepared for you from the foundation of the world. For I was hungry and you gave me food.

ALL: Amen.

PRESIDER: I was thirsty and you gave me drink . . .

ALL: Amen.

PRESIDER: . . . a stranger and you welcomed me. . .

ALL: Amen.

PRESIDER: . . . naked and you clothed me . . .

ALL: Amen.

PRESIDER: . . . ill and you cared for me . . .

ALL: Amen.

PRESIDER: . . . In prison and you visited me.

ALL: Amen.

Presider lowers his arms.

COMMENTATOR: Then the just will answer him and say, "Lord, when did we see you hungry and feed you, or thirsty and give you drink? When did we see you a stranger and welcome you, or naked and clothe you? When did we see you ill or in prison, and visit you?"

PRESIDER: "Amen, I say to you, as often as you did this for one of the least, you did this for me."

ALL: Amen.

The Hospitality Ministers come individually to Presider for blessing.

PRESIDER places both hands on head for a silent blessing.

Hospitality Ministers respond "Amen" after blessing and return to the Presider's right.

PRESIDER: [Raising hands in blessing over assembly]

We are all called to feed, clothe, welcome and love. "Amen, I say to you, as often as you do this for one of the least, you do this for me."

ALL: Amen.

PRESIDER invites everyone to stand for the Creed as Hospitality Ministers return to seats.

Hospitality Ideas

1. Ushers and greeters should be assigned to each Mass

2. Eucharistic Ministers can exercise their hospitality ministry as they gather in the back of the church before Mass.

3. In preparation for the Sunday readings, scripture texts for the following Sunday can be published in the bulletin.

4. As Ministers of Hospitality within the assembly, we can sit in the front, filling in the seats so the back pews can seat latecomers. Ushers can encourage people to move to the front so latecomers can be easily seated.

5. As "custodians of the stillness," ushers should not seat people during times of prayer, reading or the homily. Latecomers can be seated:

   a. after opening prayer, before first reading? (if so, Lector would wait till all are seated.)
   b. after the Gospel, while people are sitting for the homily.
   c. when people sit for the preparation of the gifts.

6. Ministers of Hospitality should meet regularly:

   a. to arrange scheduling,
   b. to develop plans for hospitality activities,
   c. for mutual support and prayer.

7. The Ministry of Hospitality should have one or two co-ordinators and someone responsible for scheduling ushers and greeters.

8. Start a hospitality fund (spare change jar?) for food, environment, pamphlets, and . . .?

9. Bulletin board or kiosk for annoucements, prayers for the sick, people needing rides, child care or other needs.

10. Create a welcoming environment in the Gathering Area.

11. Develop a Job Description for the Ministry of Hospitality.

Bibliography

Bernardin, Joseph Cardinal. *Our Communion, Our Peace, Our Promise: Pastoral Letter on the Liturgy.* Chicago: Liturgy Training Publications, 1984.

Buckley, Francis J. *Reconciling.* Notre Dame: Ave Maria Press, 1981.

Cieslak, William. "Hospitality." *Liturgical Institute,* Diocese of Oakland. Cassette, 1984.

Dallen, James. *Gathering for Eucharist: A Theology of Sunday Assembly.* Old Hickory: Pastoral Arts Associates of North America, 1983.

DeBoy, James J., *Getting Started in Adult Religious Education.* New York: Paulist Press, 1979.

Deiss, Lucien. *Springtime of the Liturgy.* Translated by Matthew O'Connell. Collegeville: The Liturgical Press, 1979.

Dobson, Theodore E. *Say But the Word: How the Lord's Supper Can Transform Your Life.* New York: Paulist Press, 1984.

Dunning, James B. *Ministries: Sharing God's Gifts.* Winona: Saint Mary's Press, 1985.

Eliot, T.S. "Little Gidding." *The Art of T.S. Eliot,* ed. Helen Gardner. New York: E.P. Dutton and Company, 1950.

Gelineau, Joseph. *Learning to Celebrate.* Washington, D.C.: The Pastoral Press, 1985.

Gusmer, Charles. "Is the Mass a Meal?" *Catholic Update.* Cincinnati: St. Anthony Messenger Press, 1977.

Guzie, Tad. "Reclaiming the Eucharist." *Liturgy: Central Symbols* 7, no. 1 (1987): 29-33.

Henry, Rev. James and Long, Sr. Barbara. *Interview* by author, 10 June 1987. Santa Cruz, California.

Hovda, Robert W. *Strong, Loving and Wise.* Collegeville: The Liturgical Press, 1985.

Irwin, Kevin W. *Liturgy, Prayer and Spirituality.* New York: Paulist Press, 1984.

Keifer, Ralph A. *To Hear and Proclaim.* Washington, D.C.: National Association of Pastoral Musicians, 1983.

Kuehn, Regina. "A Climate of Hospitality." Liturgy 80, 13 (April 1982): 8-10.

Lectionary for Mass. New York: Catholic Book Publishing Company, 1970.

Lopresti, Rev. James. "What Kind of Rite does the Church Want?" *North American Forum on the Catechumenate.* Asilomar, California, 22 May 1987.

Mauck, Marchita. "Rites at the Closing of a Liturgy." *Liturgy: The Rites of Gathering and Sending Forth* 1,4 (1981): 73-79.

Nouwen, Henri J.M. *Reaching Out.* Garden City: Image Books, 1975.

Powell, Karen Hinman. "Preparing a Catechumenate Team and Ministries of the RCIA." *North American Forum on the Catechumenate.* Asilomar, California, 18 May 1987.

Power, David N. *Gifts that Differ: Lay Ministries Established and Unestablished.* New York: Pueblo Publishing Company, 1980.

Rahner, Karl. "The Theology of the Symbol." *A Rahner Reader,* ed. Gerald A. McCool. New York: Seabury Press, 1975.

Rouillard, Philippe. "From Human Meal to Christian Eucharist." *Living Bread, Saving Cup,* ed. R. Kevin Seasoltz. Collegeville: The Liturgical Press, 1982.

Smith, Gregory F. *The Ministry of Ushers.* Collegeville: The Liturgical Press, 1980.

Smits, Kenneth, "A Congregational Order of Worship." *Living Bread, Saving Cup*, ed. R. Kevin Seasoltz. Collegeville: The Liturgical Press, 1982.

Szews, George R. "Ministers of Hospitality and Greeting." *Liturgy: The Rites of Gathering and Sending Forth* 1,4 (1981): 18-21.

The Sacramentary, trans. ICEL. New York: Catholic Book Publishing Company, 1985.

Vatican II, *Constitution on the Sacred Liturgy*. Washington, D.C.: United States Catholic Conference, 1964.

Walsh, Eugene A. "Hospitality: Heartbeat of Participation." *Modern Liturgy* 12 (March 1985): 5.

Walsh, Eugene A. *The Order of Mass: Guidelines*. Glendale: Pastoral Arts Associates of North America, 1979.

White, James F. "Coming Together in Christ's Name." *Liturgy: The Rites of Gathering and Sending Forth* 1,4 (1981): 7-10.

Willimon, William H. "The Peace of God Go with You." *Liturgy: The Rites of Gathering and Sending Forth* 1,4 (1981): 66-71.